To Iris Huang
    A beloved Ch...

From: Immanuel Choir
        Christmas 1988

D1000928

HANDS ACROSS THE SEASONS

Hands Across

the Seasons

Gloria Sickal Gaither
Dorothy Sickal
Suzanne Gaither
Amy Gaither

ABINGDON PRESS   Nashville

Hands Across the Seasons

Copyright © 1988 by Gloria Gaither

All rights reserved.
No part of this work may be reproduced or transmitted in any form or by any means, electronic or mechanical, including photocopying and recording, or by any information storage or retrieval system, except as may be expressly permitted by the 1976 Copyright Act or in writing from the publisher. Requests for permission should be addressed in writing to Abingdon Press, 201 Eighth Avenue South, Nashville, TN 37202.

This book is printed on acid-free paper.

Library of Congress Cataloging-in-Publication Data

Hands across the seasons / Gloria Sickal Gaither . . . [et al.].
    p. cm.
  ISBN 0-687-16578-4 (alk. paper)
  1. American poetry—Women authors. 2. American poetry—20th century. 3. Christian poetry. American. 4. Mothers and daughters--Poetry. 5. Women—Poetry. I. Gaither, Gloria.
PS589.H36   1988
811'.5'08—dc19   87-33683
                                                                                 CIP

Lines from "An Honest Lullaby" by Joan Baez © 1977, 1979 by Gabriel Earl Music. Used by permission.

Copyright information for individual poems is on pages 143-144.

MANUFACTURED BY THE PARTHENON PRESS AT
NASHVILLE, TENNESSEE, UNITED STATES OF AMERICA

To Margaret Effie Boster, Alice Floyd Sickal, Addie Hartwell, Blanche and Lela Gaither, and all the rest of the strong, pioneering women who preceded us and nurtured our parents and who reach even now across centuries of seasons to gift us with the costly heritage of opportunity for becoming all God meant for us to be.

It is the child in us who plays;
Who sees no happiness beyond today's;
Who sings for joy; who wonders, and who weeps;
It is the child in us at night who sleeps.
It is the child who silent turns his face,
Open and maskless, naked of defense,
Simple with trust, distilled of all pretense,
To sudden beauty in another's face—

*It is the child in us who loves.**

*From "The Man and the Child" by Anne Morrow Lindbergh. Copyright © 1951 by Anne Morrow Lindbergh. Reprinted from THE UNICORN AND OTHER POEMS by Anne Morrow Lindbergh, by permission of Pantheon Books, a Division of Random House, Inc.

CONTENTS

Seasons of Celebration   85

Seasons of Believing   109

I Am a Daughter and a Mother

I am a daughter and a mother, a woman sandwiched between two supercharged generations. Product of one, producer of the other, yet somehow I am the beneficiary of them both. I share my niche in history with a generation of women in transition, a painful and glorious generation, pivotal in the evolution of women.

I was born soon after bombs hit Pearl Harbor and not long before Korea became more than a tiny spot on a history classroom map. I remember when Eisenhower was president and pop music had words everyone could understand. In junior high I wore white bucks with crew socks, skirts with sewn-down pleats, and my hair in a pageboy or a ponytail. I began to become a woman when being on the honor roll was an honor and when drug addiction was only a whispered rumor about some middle-aged woman who lived "down in Riverview." I remember hula-hoops and the jitterbug, and I got good at roller skating because "Christians didn't dance." But in my heart, I danced . . . and sang and fell in love with life.

I entered college just as the decade of the fifties began to be swept into the churning, turbulent tides of the sixties. My boyfriends began to worry about being sent to Vietnam; my girlfriends worried about contraceptives; and our parents worried about us. When I went home from campus to visit, I took my dirty laundry, the latest college jargon, and my paper on existentialism. I found myself humming "If I Had a Hammer," dreaming about joining the Peace Corps, and crusading for civil rights. Just when I was making one of the biggest decisions of my life—the decision to commit myself to marriage—I heard on the evening news about the Bay of Pigs fiasco. I held my breath with all the world to see whether the bungled affair would ignite a worldwide conflagration between the two great superpowers. This was the climate in which I planned my future.

Our first child was born the week the devoted missionary,

Dr. Paul Carlson, was martyred in the Congo. And it was that August, while Watts burned on the other side of the country, that Suzanne made her first effort to walk to the other side of the room. Four years later, our second little girl took her first gulp of earth's air as satellites transmitted the voice of the first man ever to walk on the moon, claiming a "giant step for mankind."

Our son came into the world in which LSD was given to college students by their instructors as a "religious experience" and in which America held the dubious honor of giving the lives of more young soldiers than ever before in history to an undeclared war that could never be won.

> I look around and I wonder
> How the years and I survived
> I had a mother who sang to me,
> An honest lullaby.

Mother was a renegade, always wild and free even though she stayed and lived in a very structured framework. I learned from her that no one could ever steal my mind unless I was an accomplice. I saw her clean house, fix meals, and serve like a slave at times to the childish demands of immature parishioners; yet, all the while her heart and mind reigned free and regal as a queen. No one exacted service from her; no one levied the tax on her energies. She *gave*, always remaining master of herself and maintaining the privilege of choosing to give herself away. She knew bondage was first and always a slavery of the mind, and she determined always to choose whom she would call her Lord.

She knew that poverty could only be a condition of the spirit and had nothing to do with the possession of material things. She felt that when the soul was satisfied and the spirit nourished, a sort of confident opulence poured itself into one's life. One became a creator, not a consumer, a contributor instead of a user. So although we never had much money, I was not aware of being poor. Indeed, I wasn't poor. Mother clothed me extravagantly with her creativity, decorated our home with a designer's flair, and filled our lives with activities that drew friends like flies. Our home pulsated with life, and of all good things, there was more than enough.

Her writing, like her life, soars free in thought, yet is confined within the structure someone else defined. The structure could have its pound of flesh. Never mind. The form was never to be chosen over substance. Concessions always could be made to style. Oh, but the content! Content was the thing worth fighting for. Thoughts were not the prisoner of the rhyme. Thoughts of power could bring form to its knees and make it serve the thinker's end. The structure would be victim of the substance, ideas so grand and bright that no puny form could block its light, cause its eclipse.

Mother is a fighter. She is strong in will and character, absolutely fearless in the face of evil when she is convinced that right is on her side. I think she would take on any army of devils, but has a healthy respect for Satan as a living entity; she never allowed us to make light of his reality or to toy with spiritism. Yet, she taught us that the weakest believer has power over all the forces of hell when we speak and claim the name of Jesus.

She is just as fearless in the face of daily obstacles. I never remember her saying, "I can't" or "I don't know how." When something needed to be done, she assumed that there was a way to do it. And if there is a way, she will find it! She has little patience with complainers and a firm belief in ingenuity and plain old hard work. Her language is colorful, peppered with hyperbole, simile, and metaphor. She has the insight of a poet, the eye of an artist, and the persuasion of an orator. As a child, I was often her solitary audience when she unleashed a discourse on life. She didn't mind sermonizing and totally rejected the new child psychologists' view that parenting should be non-directive.

She was just as direct in her role in the church. She never considered herself "the minister's wife," but a minister herself, accountable to God for her calling, not just her husband's. She felt that any minister's wife would fail and would eventually drag her husband with her unless she herself felt a deep responsibility for serving God with what He'd given her, with or without her husband. Only then, she believed, could she handle all the pressures the parsonage life would bring and not be assailed by resentment.

It was not only ministers' wives who had to feel accountable to God, but each Christian was to be on a mission as well. I, too, as a child felt this demand for accountability. I was daily made aware of my unique abilities and talents, not just flattered and artificially "built up," but made aware of things that were really there inside me. At the same time, I was constantly reminded that "to whom much is given, much is required." I was responsible and would one day stand before God to give an account of what I did to develop and use what God had given me.

Mother was a confronter. I knew I couldn't con her or avoid her. She had eyes in the back of her head, but those eyes were not just for seeing my failures and mistakes. They were more often for seeing some spark of genius, some glimmer of beauty, some splash of creativity. She always caught me when I did something sneaky, but she caught me, too, when I did things right. She didn't brag on me or condemn me. She, instead, let me know that I was exemplifying or failing to live up to what she knew I was capable of, holding up my last best achievement as my own new standard for myself. She knew the difference between a transgression chosen out of bad motives and errors in immature judgment. During my adolescence, she often assured me that she trusted me implicitly, but did not always trust the changes in my body chemistry and my mercuric emotions at this time in my life. I felt that she was on my side, encouraging and wanting the best and highest in me to win out. Often she reminded me that I could always call home, that avoiding a trap was a courageous and intelligent thing to do. Most of all, she kept me aware of the Holy Spirit's presence in my life to give wisdom and direction when I couldn't see clearly.

I always had the feeling growing up that Mother belonged to us kids more than she belonged to the adult world. Oh, she was classy and could function with grace in sophisticated circles, but I always felt that she had a secret conspiracy with us; when grown-ups' backs were turned, she was really one of us again. We went along with her when she played at being grown-up and covered for her when we needed to. Once she showed us how to light firecrackers in the backyard of the parsonage, and the police came by to confiscate them. None of us was sure just which kinds were legal, so when the officer warned us children that the ones we'd brought home to Michigan from Indiana were not permitted, we never said a word to implicate Mother—who was busy by then pulling weeds from the iris bed.

Once my sister and I had a pajama party. It was late when Mother called upstairs in her sternest voice, "You girls go to sleep now. It's too late for any more nonsense!" Knowing that she usually meant what she said, we had all snuggled down and begun to doze when someone felt water drops on her bed. We began to stir again and whisper to one another. Soon we felt more water drops. Finally, someone got up and tiptoed to the open window. There was Mother, standing in the backyard in her nightgown, spraying us with the garden hose through the second-story window. We burst into giggles and ran downstairs, only to find a great dishpan full of hot fresh popcorn waiting for us in the summer kitchen. We all sat in a circle on the kitchen floor in the dark as Mother told us ghost stories she remembered from her childhood in the Ozarks.

Her gift for being a kid made her a great storyteller, and our little town was rich with tales that captured her imagination. Some, like the one she wove into this poem, needed little embellishment.

Old Lady Grisemar

Old Lady Grisemar lived down the road
All alone, and she shouldered the load
Of cutting her wood and planting the field;
She lived on whatever the land could yield.
Folks would drive right past her gate,

So she worked and toiled and slept and ate
And canned and washed, nighttime and morn
With no one to help her when calves were born.
A neighbor, one day passing by,
Thought she would stop and just say, "Hi!"
Grisemar responded in a friendly way,
So she asked, "How long have you lived this way—
In this lonely house from day to day?"
"Twenty years," she said, scratching her head.
"That's how long my husband's been dead.
He was mean and lazy; he would not work.
Even at talking, he managed to shirk.
He would not feed his horses hay,
And I just got tired of living that way.
So I killed him one day and threw him in the well—
I never told it, and I never will!"

The story got told far and wide,
And people laughed to split a side.
"That poor old woman, senile and crazy—"
But some remembered he was quite lazy.
He disappeared one day, they said,
And it was assumed he really was dead.
He got enough of the nagging from Nell,
So he ran away—she never would tell.

On the day she was ninety, Mrs. Grisemar died.
No one rejoiced, but nobody cried.
A bright young farmer bought her place.
He cut the weeds, and worked to replace
The broken windows, and I must tell,
He hired a crew to clean out the well.
He wanted fresh and sparkling water
For his lovely wife and little daughter.
They dug up the dry and dusty rocks,
Wire, cans, and discarded socks.
They patched the crack in the cistern's side,
And he rode down a rope, and there he found

A pile of bones, half hid in the ground.
At last they learned as sure as—well,
She *did* kill her husband and throw him in the well.

—Dorothy Sickal

Yes, Mother taught me how to laugh, sometimes at life, sometimes at myself. She always saw the funny things in church, and she knew I wasn't being irreverent when I saw them, too. She saw Susie, tired and overworked by her family, fall asleep just as she was subconsciously reaching to adjust the veil on her perennial black hat. Somehow, Susie caught her index finger in the webbing, and as she nodded, the finger dangled, suspended in the air. Lower and lower Susie's head fell until the dangling hand touched her knee and nudged her toward consciousness. Back upright, her head snapped, but Susie could not get quite awake enough to realize that her hand was caught and hanging in midair. The whole youth group was convulsed with laughter by the time the final amen was given.

Laughter, tears, commitment, responsibility, liberation, devotion, loyalty, and discernment—these are only a few of the gifts my mother has given me. Her writing reflects these attributes, and it constantly reminds me of my awesome heritage.

Now, how can I describe the threads woven into my life by these amazing people I call my *children*? To speak of them as children calls to most minds an image of "charges" over which a parent is caretaker. It summons visions of midnight vigils, endless grocery shopping, cooking, bedmaking, laundry, instructions, lectures, discipline, and advice. While it is true that all of these are a part of mothering a growing family, that picture is not adequate to describe the relationship my daughters and I share. As the years sift away, I come to recognize that it is, in fact, not so different from the relationship I have had with my mother, that of comrades in a private club to which we all belong.

I remember when I was a child building "club houses" in the

corner of the schoolyard, in old deserted chicken coops or in half-broken sheds. My friends and I would dream up some name to call our club, invent secret codes, and paint our exclusive insignia on the clubhouse door. Together we would pledge our energies to solving neighborhood mysteries, making ambitious plans, and dreaming grand dreams.

Such is the impression that remains of my life-long relationship with my mother and my daughters. We have built a sort of private club house in our spirits, and even when we go about the tasks of living in the "outside world" we can always count on this special group to share our dreams, to pick us up when we fall, to laugh when we're joyous, to cry when we hurt, and always, always to believe we *can*—even when to all the world one of us looks like a loser.

The coded messages of our secret club have often been poems left on the kitchen counter, mailed to camp or home from college, pasted to the bathroom mirrors, or even skewered on the twig of a pine tree.

Our "meetings" have been held in nurseries, under willow trees, in rowboats, at sophisticated dinners, in church, at the town bakery, on bicycles, in buses, at picnic tables, in a cabin in the woods, and beside the creek. These have been our makeshift club houses, places where we have met in secret, "snuck off" to share some news, laughed in delight over some accomplishments, or just to be still together and listen to the quiet.

My daughters, too, have taught me. They have taught me to greet life with open arms and to look at life straight on, eye to eye. No matter how often I fail or make errors in judgment, they seem to forgive everything at sunset and give me a brand new start at dawn. They see people with their hearts and not just with their eyes. They see beauty that transcends age and greatness in common folk. They have taught me that there is a difference between hype and hope and that hype is what people settle for when there is no hope.

They have taught me that as a mother and as a person, I don't have to be God; I just need to be real. Mistakes I will make, but children are the world's best examples of grace, always giving not what we deserve but what we need. Because they see us as we really are and not as society defines us, they seem to sense sooner exactly what we need.

When I have been least lovable, Amy has often surprised me with a hug. When I am most exhausted, I find Suzanne picking up the load emotionally, spiritually, and physically without a word, without my asking. When life gets too complicated, one of them has been there to make me laugh or to coax me into stopping for a cup of coffee or a walk along the creek.

So it is that my children have given me a better understanding of what God is like—always calling out the best in me, stripping away the sham, forgiving me when I have failed, lifting my load when I am burdened with life, and changing my focus when the world is too much with me. Grace, redemption, forgiveness, and tough love—these my children have taught me.

My children have been my friends and have given me an excuse to be myself. They have given me a reason to run barefoot down beaches, sled down snowy hillsides, climb trees, catch fireflies on warm summer evenings, and fly kites across Indiana meadows. They have shared my delight in all first things: the first snowflake of the winter, the first star at night, the first apple blossom in the spring, the first robin to sing, the first plunge into the ocean, the first tomato from the garden, and the first ride each year in our convertible.

They have saved me from cynicism and taught me to accept people and circumstances in my life with openness, reserving judgment until I have all the facts. They have shown me how to take each day as it comes and, as the scripture directs, not to borrow worries from tomorrow, for today is sure to have enough worries of its own.

Most of all, I have learned that in the family of God we are all siblings, and that that relationship supersedes all others. Before I am my daughters' mother, I am their sister. Before my daughters are my mother's grandchildren, they are her sisters. In the primary relationship of life, we are all kids under construction and, in a very real way, we are each responsible for how the other "turns out."

I Am a Daughter and a Mother ⸭ 17

I have discovered from my mother and from my daughters that we all have the same needs: to be accepted, to be praised and appreciated, to be able to trust without fear of betrayal, to be understood, to be listened to, not to be taken for granted, to be hugged and noticed. These needs know no generation gap, and because of them we really do need one another.

Together we are bound by our commitment to something and to Someone that transcends generations, that transcends eons of time. We are branches of the Family tree, branches of the true vine. It is only in union with the Vine that we branches and twigs can give one another nourishment. Perhaps Amy has expressed it best in her poem "Branches."

Branches

You have formed us . . .
Shaped us from clay,
Molded our minds,
Planted our hearts,
Created our souls,
And set us forth—
Loved
And free.
We are only what you have made us to be;
Creatures in your kingdom,
Lovely, complex, capable,
And full of Promise.
Yet, so many of us
Turn away . . .
Forget how to love,
Or never knew . . .
We are the branches,
The extension of you—
We fail.
We fall.
We forget.
We are living Breaths . . .

Breathing Souls!
Alive . .
And so full.
Teach us to follow—
And to lead.
Teach us to listen—
And to hear.
Teach us to reach—
And to love.

For
You have formed us.

Amy Gaither at eighteen

Portions of the text of this section first appeared in "She Sang Me an Honest Lullaby," by Gloria Gaither, in the Spring 1983 issue of *Today's Christian Woman*, a publication of Christianity Today, Inc.

Seasons of
Becoming

Aspirations

Mary wanted to be a writer.
Tom wanted to run the world.
Sue wanted to have a mansion.
Jim wanted to own the girls.

Mary grew to become a teacher.
Tom runs the grocery store.
Sue's a wife and has a baby.
Jim's alone and very poor.

I want to be a writer. . . .

Suzanne Gaither at sixteen

You Walked So Straight

You walked so straight tonight
You didn't even wobble
On your new high heels.
And you sure earned the honor
The way you've planned your time,
Made sacrifices,
Followed through.
I'm proud of you,
Although sometimes I'm scared
Of what you might
And might not
Become.

You're so responsible.
Sometimes I feel that I'm YOUR child.
I watch with open admiration
While you make good choices
And tough decisions
And never look back.
But you do look ahead.
You've calculated every course
So you won't waste a bit
Of your potential.

I'm glad that you're the way you are—
I told you you were special—
Yet when I saw your slender hands,
Curled childlike 'round your cheek
Last night,
You there, asleep,
I felt my heart still wanting to hold on
And wishing you still needed the support
Of my own hand,
For deep inside I know
That when I do let go

Your strength will take you far;
Yet let you go I will
And feel the thrill of knowing you can fly.

I'll spend my winter's springs
Remembering.
The heart is a good place to keep things.

Gloria Gaither

To Be an Artist

I want to touch,
Touch hearts that need to be touched.
I want to feel,
Feel for those who want compassion.
I want to communicate,
Communicate to those who need recognition.
I want to understand,
Understand those who ache to be understood.
And I want to be understood
By those who wish to understand.

I want to love,
Love those who don't know what love is,
Those who want love,
Those who think they don't.

I do not wish for fame or notoriety—
To be a "star"—
I want to be an artist.

Amy Gaither at fifteen

To Be a Dreamer

It is a curse, of sorts,
To be born a dreamer,
To believe with all you are
In what is not yet
And know that there is more
Beyond the now than ever has been;
To see, in all that dashes,
What one has
To bits upon the rocks,
Insistent hope arising from the mist.
Alas, to be a dreamer
Makes one a misfit in this world.
It stirs the inner soul
With discontent at status quo
While others seek in it
Contentment.
It makes one satisfied, instead,
With what life offers unsolicited,
Yet spells boredom to a world
That will achieve at any cost.
A dreamer is a thorn in the flesh
Of systems and structures
And on a given day may enrage
Society with too many questions
Or remain silent and detached
When answers are demanded
To help increase production
Or stabilize some bottom line.
A dreamer's not a painless thing to be;
Dreams are insistent masters
That will not let their servant rest
But urge and disturb
And call for an accounting of each moment
In the perfect ledger of eternity.
So, caught between the dream

And this brash earth,
The dreamer finds no rest and little comfort.
And the further from the energy and innocence
Of childhood the dreamer grows,
The oftener he's apt to pray
That dreams may die a bit.

Gloria Gaither

One Mother's Prayer

Sing me no eulogy of praise.
Give me no hallowed stool;
Just let me be my children's friend,
Their bulwark in life's school.

Don't make of me a gilded queen
Or unsophisticated clod,
But let me understand their needs,
And point their way to God.

Help me to live the things I preach,
Admit my faults and fears.
O let me be humble enough
To blend with theirs my tears.

Let me be firm to earn their trust,
Not gullible or weak.
Let my child know I care enough
To mean it when I speak!

This world needs mothers with a goal,
Unswayed by changing fad,
Who love the Lord and by his grace,
Can tell good from the bad.

I seek no sentimental crown,
No high and lofty praise,
But give me children who will stand
Through these ungodly days.

The greatest "thank you" I could ask,
Most satisfying pay,
Will come when they are at Christ's side
On God's great Judgment Day!

Dorothy Sickal

Union of Poles

The mind
The caldron behind the eyes
Bubbles as it muses
Leaps and then diffuses
Laughs before it cries
Bubbles up
Like little dogs
Chasing
  Biting
    Hiding
      Fighting
        Dying
Giving birth
Engaging in the noble art
Of building fences 'round the heart
Then tearing them away
In reconciliation
A kind of Yom Kippur
Two giant, groping hands
In Darkness clasp at last
Illuminating worlds unknown
They stare into the eyes of Fate
With sharp stilettos piercing through
Defying her with silent blasts
And like a beaten bully cowers
She shyly turns her head to leave
And gives to those who would believe
(With unity of heart and mind)
The right to stand with fists clenched tight
And scream into the sky

"I think . . . No. I believe it so!
Yes, I know!
    I KNOW!"

Suzanne Gaither at twenty

Identity

The face of a petunia
Is a wondrous thing,
Poised toward the light—
Delicate, ruffled—
Holding up its horn
For water, pollen, honey.

Their faces unashamed,
Yet their open admission of themselves
Does not diminish their loveliness,
They are. That's all.
They function. That's all.
They don't pretend to be duller
Or brighter
Than they are.
They don't have to bow their heads
Or hide their glorious faces
So that the geraniums
Will feel whole and confident.
They simply shine
And grow on to open fully
And complete their total cycle
With never a downward glance.
And when their time is finished
And their prime a wilted memory,
They fold the wrinkled membranes
Of all that they have been
Around their very souls
And make from them
The seed of what is yet to be.
At last they spill the dregs of life
Into the waiting soil
And are transformed into
The hope of new beginnings.

Gloria Gaither

Perception

Do not picture me in buildings
Made of brick
And mortar
By hard hands.
Do not think of me
Bound by rules,
Trapped by old ideas
And meaningless ritual.
Do not remember me
Serious and grim,
Intent on things
And discontent with life.

Picture me in fields of white daisies
And yellow buttercups,
Clothed in clouds of misty white
With radiant face and hands of love.
Think of me
With wings of light,
Freeing me to dance
And sing in joyous tones,
Unafraid to fly
And unbound by structure.

Remember me laughing
The carefree laughter of a life well loved
With arms outstretched
Waiting to embrace
And be loved—

For this is the image
I wish to see
Of myself

Amy Gaither at seventeen

Of Course!
(for Benjy)

During the storm and the sailing,
 Jonah did not see the whale;
Though he strained his eyes in the darkness
 Not a nose, not a fin, not a tail!
Of course, he was not looking
 For a big, black, blubbery whale!

His main concern was escaping
 From the presence and sight of God,
As if to dismiss his Creator
 With a wink or a kick or a nod.
Of course, God could make Jonah obey him
 Without a word or a frown or a rod.

So Jonah napped while a'tossing
 On the wild and foamy sea.
He must have thought, "I'll escape him
 If I close my mind, you see."
Of course, he never imagined
 All the places that God can be!

He never dreamed of involving
 A host of his fellowmen
In the awful mess he was making
 By the rot and the plot of his sin.
Of course, they soon learned the trouble
 And demanded an answer from him.

Ole Jonah started a'sweatin'
 And he squirmed and fretted and cried.
"Throw me out!" he finally shouted.
 For this, he would rather have died.
Of course, it would have been better
 To obey his God than to hide.

That submarine-whale was awaiting
  For a morsel of food to eat,
So he swallowed up "Jon" like mackerel,
  And he landed inside on his feet!
Of course, in all that blackness
  Poor Jonah experienced defeat.

But he also saw God a'making
  A way for him to repent,
So he screamed for help from his Maker,
  And thus his rebellion was spent.
Of course, his sin made the whale sick
  So up on the shore he went.

This time he landed a'runnin'
  To preach the Word to the poor;
He still had to learn a few lessons
  But he never did *that* anymore!!
Of course, to obey in the first place
  Always minuses griefs by the score.

Dorothy Sickal

Oasis

We read these poems
And pick them apart
In order that we might "understand" them.
We analyze them
And their creators
And then we take the test
And move on.
But I read them—
I listen
And I hear.
I hear the creator—
I see him and feel him
And I understand him.
Not because I analyze him,
Certainly not because I listen
To those around me . . .
But because the poet is a part of me.
I feel these words;
I hang on to them
And fall behind the others around me.

I read them again—
I listen.
I hear not only their creators,
But their Creator;
And then I run to this paper
And listen.

I hear my own poem,
And it is my refuge.

Amy Gaither at sixteen

Hope

I marvel at the way
That hope keeps breaking through;
There's some kind of living, growing thing
Inside of me.
In spite of empty words
And plastic days
That tell me that I don't exist,
I do exist!
In spite of everything,
I cannot be content to die!
It is the Life in me
That keeps on reenacting
Resurrection.

Gloria Gaither

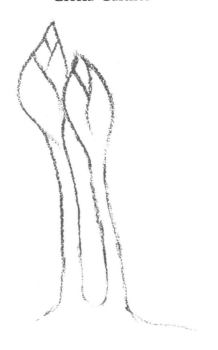

The Void

Empty nonexistence
Before catharsis
Before yellow essence
Urgent, breathless
Spews into space
Into time
And timeless, vivid, brilliant
Covers, coats, erases
From vacuum to meaning
From indecision to direction
From obscurity to substance
Bursting into oblivion

And there was . . .
   There was . . . LIGHT

   Suzanne Gaither at twenty-one

Progeria

I know what it's like
To grow old before you live.
To be withered,
Drained out,
Used up.
There was so much
I once thought I could do.
So many dreams.
So few doubts.
Today I feel
As if I've passed the summit
To find my dreams just silly fantasy
And the abilities to make them live,
Just empty mirages.
My days are leaking out
Through all the holes
In my self-confidence,
Wasted fluids on infertile land.
I've tricked myself
With colorful cosmetics,
But today
My face is clean,
And I am old.

Gloria Gaither

Equilibrium

I dropped a glass today,
And it shattered into a million pieces,
But the bird outside my window went right
  on singing,
As if there were no other noise in the world.

I failed a test today
(Though I'm used to passing),
But the sun went right on shining,
As if nothing could ever darken the sky again.

I saw a sparrow die today,
But the wind went right on blowing,
Just as if the hard little body
Wasn't already cold enough.

My shirt ripped today,
Right over my heart,
But the sun didn't stop shining,
And the birds didn't stop singing,
And the breeze didn't stop blowing;
They just went right on. . . .

                    Amy Gaither at fifteen

To Know a Heart

To sit upon a rock and wonder
Why the sea comes to the shore
And feel the wind's cool breezes blowing
And touch the sandy ocean floor,
To behold the blackness of the coral
And the whiteness of the cranes,
And know a heart that has no prison
And a mind that has no chains.

To watch a farmer's fingers putting
Tiny seeds into the ground,
Then take small clumps of moist, black sod
And cover them without a sound
And see each tiny seed mature
To healthy stalks of golden grain,
And know a heart that has no prison
And a mind that has no chains.

To feel the mighty roar of thunder
Then see white lightning by and by
And feel the hand of God himself
Shake the earth and split the sky
Then hear the quiet pitter-patter
Of tiny, tear-shaped drops of rain,
And know a heart that has no prison
And a mind that has no chains.

When theories of the world around me
Rip apart what I believe,
Decaying morals of society
Try to trick me, lie, deceive—
Still I function unaffected,
Knowing I've not lived in vain,
For I know a heart that has no prison
And a mind that has no chains.

                    Suzanne Gaither at seventeen

The Pilgrim

You said we'd go from strength to strength—
I hold to that,
Although today it feels
As if the graph of me
Would look more like it goes
From weakness to weakness.

In fact, I keep discovering weaknesses
I didn't know I had,
And old ones that I thought I'd conquered long ago
Sneak back into my days
In little subtle ways:
The tendency under pressure
To say "I can't" and give it up;
The impulse to run away,
To hide behind the talents I don't have
And shout about them loudly enough
To evade the ones I do;
The way I get excited about something far away
And spend enormous energy
In the planning,
But when it comes to doing
What I know to do today,
I do the grocery shopping instead
And call it noble and necessary,
Knowing all the while
My world is full of real people
Who can't live by bread alone.

So often I won't risk the hassle.
I'd rather have folks like me
Than to be a fool for Your sake.
I can't stand it when I hear "that pushy dame,"
So I betray my own potential
And squander what You gave
And blame it on "the times."

Yet still, in spite of everything,
When I look back at where I've been,
I see that what I am becoming
Is a whole lot further down the road
From where I was.

I'm learning how to love
  with grit
To hope
  with muscle
To live
  with joy.
And when I fail or win,
I'm learning not to build three tabernacles
And stay there.
And though the tasks that lie ahead
Loom high before me like tall Everest,
When I look back, I see
I've left behind some foothills climbed,
And they are beautiful
In the dawn
Of this new day.

Gloria Gaither

Peripeteia*

We were three in a blaze
Seven times hungry
When from death's dream
He appeared
Silently
With sword in hand
As if to make mute beasts
Utter some spoken Word.
I thought of Manoah,
Of ascension into
Fire that did not burn
And knew more of Peniel
Than hell.
It seems but steamy illusion,
Phasing only now from hindsight.
Limping from remembrance of time,
I almost let it pass my eyes without recognition . . .
An instant blessed by God
A night smothered by dawn
A moment kissed by eternity
When I became Israel
And emerged as Phoenix from the flame.

Suzanne Gaither at twenty-one

Peripeteia—term used in early Greek drama to mean a sudden or unexpected "reversa" or reversal; when the hero finally *sees* his mistakes, and the consequences of them, and turns his life around.

The entire poem contains biblical allusions to God's messengers (angels) who come to help people see the wrongness of their ways and turn their lives around.

The phoenix is a bird in Egyptian mythology, which arose newborn from the ashes after consuming itself by fire.

Metamorphosis

The spring is metamorphosing into summer,
And I can feel the dry and leathery skin
That encased me through the winter
Getting much too tight and troublesome
For comfort.
I want out!
Out into the fragrant breeze
That soon will dry the natal moisture
From my wings,
Out into the sun
From which I'll draw
The energy to fly.

And fly I will!
And as I soar,
I'll drink in all of life
That I can hold.
I'll saturate my mind
With sounds of love and peace,
And all around I'll see and notice
Everything that moves or breathes.
I'll smell the fragrance of the earth
And kiss the wind
And taste the brand of honey
Every blossom has to offer;
Yet I'll be sure to hear
The silence that the warm and welcome
Evening brings,
And in it I will race with shadows
Just to see which one of us
Can tiptoe in more softly
'Cross the grass.
(I'll walk so gently,
Even you won't
Hear me pass.)

And knowing as I do
The days can't last,
That winter will return too soon,
I'll do and hear and think
And taste it all!
I'll store up multicolor memories
To take me through
The long, gray days
Of winter.

Gloria Gaither

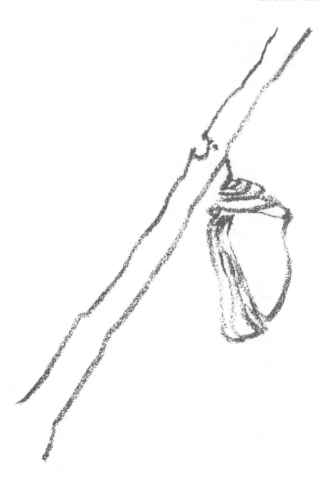

Alone

I'm not sure
  of the day
for the passing
  weeks have been
    merely
  slurs and blobs—
never night
  nor day nor
    rain nor cold
but sulking
  shadows
like blurs and globs
  of wet, black
    ink
spilling from
an aching pen.

Suzanne Gaither at twenty-two

Is This All?

If life has no more purpose
Than to fight to keep alive;
If all there is to living
Is to struggle and to strive,
Without a contribution
To some worthwhile total plan,
God went to too much trouble
Just to fashion man.

'Tis sure that there are things of earth
More beautiful than thought—
Things to eat and work to do
And joys that can't be bought.
But even this is not enough
If when we die, we're dead!
There still must be a better use
For this brain in my head.

By the time we learn to do a thing,
That page of life is turned,
And we are left without a cause
To use the thing we've learned.
O what a waste if after all,
No perfect plan comes through—
Man's talents are all scattered,
And there is nothing else to do!

I think the God so organized,
As the one I've come to know,
Would never stop the story
In the middle of the show!
The truths we learn so slowly
Must not perish with the sun,
And we will learn to use them
When this life's school is done.

We then can think unhampered
By the false, the flaws, the filth
That clog the works so often
And frustrate a world of wealth.
We can soar to heights unfathomed
When from earth's bounds we're free,
For truth will flow unshackled,
And we will really see!

Dorothy Sickal

Waters

These are the waters of disbelief . . .
And I must swim them.

Before, I could stand on the shore,
Play on the beach,
Laugh and believe
Like a child,
Because I was one.

And now, because I waited in the shallows,
I have tasted unbelief—
In my self—
In God—
In the whole Human Race.
It was bitter,
And my tears
Were the salt of the water—
My dry ache,
The sand on the shore.

Now I must swim
To the other shore
Where the New Children await me,
Laughing, believing, like the children
They once were.

These are the waters of disbelief—
And I must swim them . . .

Amy Gaither at seventeen

There Are No Puppies

There are no puppies anymore—
No frolic of little paws
Across the hillside
Through forbidden flowers,
No nipping at tender legs,
No cold, wet noses.
There are no gentle whimpers,
Crying sadly in the night
For sleeping playmates.
There are no worn and trodden paths
Around the hedges
Or balls of soft fur
Tumbling across the lawn.
No, there are no puppies anymore.
Now the grass is full and fresh,
And the fallen leaves tumble across the yard.
The night is painfully peaceful,
And the flowers have put forth
Their loveliest blooms,
But in the valley there is an empty little house.
Oh, if there were only puppies.

Suzanne Gaither at twenty

Seasons of Relationships

I Like Being Married to You

I like being married to you . . .
   I like the way you put on your socks,
   Insist on wearing your run-down, slip-on Hush Puppies
   (When everyone else is wearing tie-up Oxfords),
   Refuse to throw away your old white pants
   (Just because they have a little paint on the cuff),
   Persist in believing in people.
I like being married to a man who thinks everyone should . . .
   Plant a tree,
   Face problems squarely,
   Spend time with his own children,
   Quit smoking,
   Be himself.
I like being loved by a man . . .
   Who will tell me the truth,
   Say what he means,
   Make valid evaluations . . .
Because when you hold me close and tell me
   That you love me,
     I feel there must be something to me
      After all!

Gloria Gaither

Who Is It?

Who will be
My forever lover,
Fresh and full of light,
Burning mystery in the night
So much I cannot guess you
In a thousand years of time?
Who will be
The fury and the calm,
An agitating balm
That pushes me to heights
And holds me there?
Who are you?
And if you do exist,
Then speak your name,
And without reservation
I will run
To meet you half the way.

Suzanne Gaither at twenty

To Whom It May Concern

If time brings sweet wine
To flasks of crushed grapes,
And wounds are healed
When sands sift through narrow glass,
Then time remains my friend
And brings to me
You.

When I know the taste of the bread
Of your spirit
And my soul is
Your mate
And the vines of our love bloom,
Life will plant seeds,
And love will make fertile
The ground of our youth
And our age.
But until then,
I remain vulnerable,
Willing to walk half the distance,
Reap half the harvest.

                    Amy Gaither at seventeen

One and One Make One

We've grown to be one soul—two parts;
Our lives so intertwined
That when some passion stirs your heart,
I feel the quake in mine.

One might suspect (who'd never known
A love so pure and true)
That this would make one twice as sad
And split the joy in two.

But I have found our oneness makes
The joys flow manifold,
And sadness touched by angel wings
Is essence rich as gold.

Love cuts away the clouds with strokes
Adept as surgeon's knife,
And leaves the trusting heart aglow
With glorious love of life!

Gloria Gaither

You

I held back at first
Scars and indecision
Blocked the door
And risks, however promising and sweet,
Were not enough to sell me anymore
And so I stood my ground.
But all at once
The air turned light
And every raindrop
Filled itself with song.
Holding hands they danced
Upon once superficial ground
Laughing little children
Penetrating all the while
And so I felt
And laughed and danced along.
Yet in the midst
A humble love
Was dancing softly too
I dreamed imagination
Or so I thought
But it was you.

Suzanne Gaither at twenty

The Fighter

"Well, you can't win 'em all,"
He said with a shrug of his shoulder that day,
When the last of his dream finally crumbled away.
And he managed a bit of a lopsided grin
That gave me a hint of the greatness in him.
"I may as well quit!"
But I knew by the glint in his eye
He'd go straight as a dye to the scene of defeat,
And he'd try one more time—
It was part of his nature to try and to try—
So though his lips said, "I'm through,"
I knew what he'd do.
"You can't win 'em all . . ."

"But you can,"
Said the soul of his being,
"Win some."

And he won!

Gloria Gaither

Intuition

When intuition summons
One cannot help but follow
It assembles roads
Into that which is against mechanism
Broken steps of ancient castles
Conceal what magic lies inside
Blessings and promises
Tokens and kisses
Seal with great stones
Reason's grave
And the whisper
Of the smallest word from your lips
Leads mysteriously to your heart.

Suzanne Gaither at twenty-two

To My Mother

It seems that wherever you go,
You bring *home* with you.
You turn bare rooms
And empty containers
Into temporary nests,
Always open and warm—
And always inviting.
I find I never get quite enough time
In your home-ness,
Or enough time with you.
I am never so open
Or completely me
As when I am with you,
And though the strings
Connecting your heart to mine
Are much more than strings
And can never break,
Regardless of how far away I go.
Nothing replaces just being with you—
Quiet, talking, reading,
Writing, sleeping, sharing
Always.
The older I get, and the more I learn,
The more I realize
How precious is our friendship,
Our bond;
And I know, more and more,
That I cannot exist
Without dipping into the well
Of your companionship
And, in return, pouring out
My rich and loyal love
On you, my precious Mother.

Amy Gaither at eighteen

Sibling

I want to understand you,
but I want you to understand me, too.
I want to listen,
but I also want to be heard.
I want to love you,
but please love me back.
I want to give to you,
no matter what,
but I'm tired.
My heart hurts.
I need you
To need me.

Amy Gaither at fifteen

To Our Daughter

To your husband you are:
    A cook, housekeeper, valet, and mother;
    You are a critic, defender, and cover;
    You are companion, help-mate and lover.

To your children you are:
    The source for supplying personal needs,
    The personification of love,
    The hostess of God,
    The spoon-outer of justice,
    And the kisser of wounds.

You are the bulwark against all enemies,
A harbor wherein lies security from the storms of life.
You are the one person who does not demand
    "a pound of flesh."
You can be trusted not to discuss their faults and their failures
    with outsiders,
And your recompense for labor is always
    Intangible
        Qualitative
            Spiritual . . .

But to your parents you are:
    An answer to prayer,
    The fulfillment of a dream.
    A princess, a sparkling jewel,
    A treasure to be cherished, polished, protected—
    A charge.

You are the recipient
Of years of loving care and patient training.
No matter where you go, what you do or attain to,
It is your personal qualities, welfare, and well-being
That will be their constant concern.

You may lose your charm, beauty, faculties,
But to your parents, you will always be
Beautiful and cherished for the person inside.
We are grateful for our years of joy in your company
And your loyalty to God, which will always
   remain our goal for you.

Though the fickle world forsake you,
Your friends reject you,
And your physical beauty fade away,
Though your material blessings melt into nothingness,
To your parents you will always be—
   Beautiful,
     Lovely,
       Desirable,
         An answer to prayer,
And our little girl to be protected, nurtured,
   And, at last, presented at the throne of grace—
Ushered into the kingdom of heaven.

Dorothy Sickal

Left

"Are you leaving, Grandma?"
The child asked.
The grandmother continued talking.
"Are you leaving, Grandma?"
The child asked again.
Again there was no reply.
"Grandma, are you leaving?"
The child asked, frightened.
But the grandmother never answered
And the child never asked again
And the grandmother left.

Amy Gaither at sixteen

At the Last

"As long as I can hear the children. . . . "
Her cracked voice filtered through the screen;
The children played in the park nearby.
"I feel safe in here alone,"
She said.
Children on bikes and skates
After play
Rode away from the watermelon sunset,
But she ran toward it
With heavy eyes,
And the children
Were the last sounds she heard.

Suzanne Gaither at twenty-two

The Glory

Pale, thin moon was feebly clinging
To a dull and hazy sky
In the west while east was blazing,
Pierced with brilliant streaks of dye.

Then I heard the soft wind whisper,
Heard first chirpings of a bird;
Yet that moon, though old and sallow,
Held her place and never stirred.

So I felt within my bosom
First a pity, then disgust;
She had ruled o'er stars in glory;
Why for daybreak did she lust?

Through the night she'd moved in splendor,
Like a princess, fine as lace.
Now I saw her blue enchantment
In full daylight out of place.

Then I felt my own heart tremble,
And my fingers sought my face;
Master, in the name of heaven,
Give me grace to see my place!

Dorothy Sickal

Time for Separating

Thank God for fall—
The time for letting go
Of all for which the sowing work was done,
The labor in the sun,
The watering and weeding,
The nurture of the seedling,
And praying for the rain.
Through all the spring and summer,
The hope that made the waiting
Worth the wait
Has been anticipating
This fine day
When seedlings stood up strong
On stalks that bore the weight
Of lovely buds and blossoms
Of their own.
And all along we knew
There'd be a separating,
A time when roots reached deep
Into the soil
To nurture what we'd planted.
The labor and the toil—
That happiest of work—
Would be much less demanding,
And there'd be time for standing
In the sunset
Hand in hand.

So here it is, the fall,
The time for separating;
Yet, nothing's lost at all,
And nothing disappears
This harvest time of year;
And, yes, there's time
For savoring the joy,

For storing in the heart
And filling up the soul's wide granaries
With what has grown to be,
The fruit of finest dreams.

We sift the kernels through our hands
And sing
To find them pregnant with the spring!

Gloria Gaither

Long Distance Leaf

The Colorado leaves
turn their backs
    expecting rain,
And I think:
you once said,
    "This is Indiana—humid
        air and wind
and the leaves with their
    backs to the sky."

So unfamiliar
familiar
And I'm here
            alone
With my back to the sky

        expecting rain.

Suzanne Gaither at twenty-two

Freshman, 1987

I wept last evening
To feel the loneliness that swept the room—
The loneliness that laughed and danced
And drowned brain cells in aluminum cans
And plastic cups bearing the school insignia.
The loneliness, so silent, it nearly burst my eardrums
With its senseless screaming.

And all the time,
As I watched and wondered,
I wished I could fit . . . but not perfectly . . . somehow . . .
Stand out, just enough to be noticed
And remembered.
But last night there seemed to be
No place for me.
So I retreated
To the stillness of my room
And contemplated openings and missing pieces
And loneliness
And decided that I wasn't lonely—
Only misplaced,
Waiting to fit.

Amy Gaither at eighteen

Little Nell

When I was just a little girl,
My mother read a poem.
It impressed me so completely;
It changed my life and home.

It was all about a family
And it set about to say
How each child loved its mother
And expressed it in some way.

For most love was all verbal;
They were lavish in their praise,
But each one went his merry way
To spend the carefree days.

At last came daughter, Little Nell,
Who *really* loved her mother;
She acted what they only spoke—
Her sisters and her brother.

She swept the floor and fed the cat
And never once complained;
When all the others failed to help
She cleaned up what remained.

Her mother knew she loved her;
It was easy to believe—
She lifted many burdens
The rest could not perceive.

It is easy to sing praises
While we let emotions thrive,
But when it comes to serving,
We are only half alive.

Praise that costs us nothing
Cannot be praise at all,
And love without some action
Shows gratitude too small.

When all our prayers and praises
Concern something for ourselves,
We miss the joy and gladness
That come to "Little Nells."

Dorothy Sickal

Sunshine

Right from the start I've called you "Sunshine,"
And that's just what you are,
Sunshine, rainbows, and butterflies.

I used to try to make you frown.
"Frown, Amy," I'd say.
And then I'd laugh
To see your furled little forehead
Betrayed by your upturned grin.

You've skipped and giggled and danced
Like golden sunbeams on a rippled stream
And painted my world yellow.
You see the good in things and people—
And in me.

You understand before I ask you to.
When I am tired
Or worried
Or unfair,
You make excuses for me.

You forgive so eagerly;
It seems forgiveness is a gift
You've wrapped ahead of time and held behind
   your back
Like some delicious secret.
My needing it so
Gives you excuse to give it,
And that brings you joy.

At games you seldom win;
You don't have the heart for it.
You seem to see your winning as a way
To make a loser of your friend.

And so you choose to play at things
Where everybody wins.

You choose skating over tennis,
And when we let you pick,
It's always biking over baseball,
Unless we all agree not to keep score,
"Just play for fun."

You've been so good at losing—
I have a feeling in the end
You are the one
Who always wins, Sunshine.

Gloria Gaither

To My Gracious Mother*

How often as an ignorant picaro
I have left you collapsed by the bridge
And have ridden away in search of some holy grail.
I knew well the rules of the universe—
Even unintentional pain must be avenged—
Yet lesser men recognized purity of heart,
   singleness of mind.
I saw the unseen illusion,
   drank from the cup,
      touched the Fisherking,
But because I did not think to love,
Because of my unforgivable pride,
   which caused God himself
   to seal my mouth,
I failed to ask the questions
   that could have saved the kingdom,
And in that moment,
   which in its fragile hand clutched
   all of eternity,
Your pain began to beat in my heart;
Your sickness grabbed my bleeding throat,
And I knew that you had died
   . . . and died of grief.

                    Suzanne Gaither at twenty-two

---

*Based on the myth of the Holy Grail and the Fisherking fertility myth (which states that if the Fisherking is in bad health or dies, the entire kingdom eventually dies). Naive, irresponsible Perceval left his dear mother collapsed by the bridge, to seek the grail. Yet he was stricken mute because of his negligence, and even though he was pure in heart, he was unable to ask the questions that would have saved the kingdom.

I Know a Lady

I watch the lovely lady,
Sharing her heart with thousands.
I watch her bustling through her day;
I watch her peeling
  the onions over the sink;
I watch her, patiently, and sometimes
  not so patiently, answering the tenth call of the day
  at nine in the morning;
I watch her in one of the hundreds
  of motel rooms she has seen,
Lying quiet and exhausted in a rare and much needed
  afternoon nap before sound check;
I watch her in a secluded and carefully selected refuge,
  putting a bouquet of freshly cut seaside flowers
  into a water-filled hotel glass,
Then turn to the sleepy heads in the beds
  to announce cheerfully she's going
  for an early morning walk,
  should anyone wish to join her.

I've watched her reluctantly packing to interrupt
  her summer for an "unavoidable" departure;
I've watched her stop in the middle of writing
  grocery lists, calling J.C. PENNEY, and
  sorting through the mail
  to turn as her husband walks in the door
  and be caught up in his arms for a moment;
I've watched her cry and laugh,
Scold and be scolded,
Glow with pride and anger,
Work and play,
Succeed and fail,

Give comfort,
And break down.
But never,
NEVER
Have I seen my mother weak.

Amy Gaither at fourteen

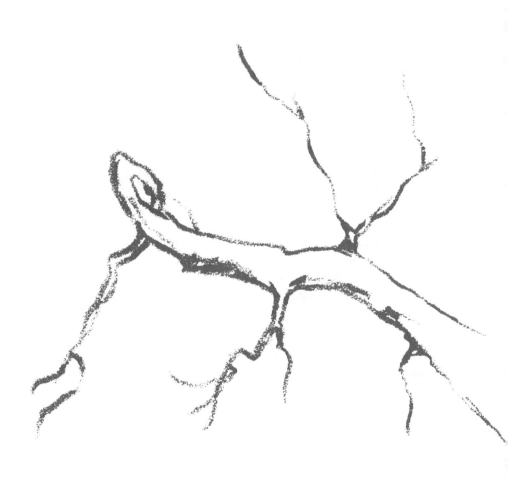

Value

You came, and you took.
You took time
and energy
  and time
and attention
  and time
and love
  and time
and elbow grease
  and time
and my sleep
  and time.
But you brought more.
  You brought sunshine
    and bubbles
    and music
    and laughter
    and sandboxes
    and playdough
    and yellow ribbons
    and flesh-colored Band-Aids
    and arpeggio scales
    and "The Waltons"
    and roller skates
    and blow-up kites
    and
    joy.
You were the best investment I ever made.

Gloria Gaither

Miscast

I'm not so good at this.
Miscast I am to play
This role.
The stage directions say
Deliver all these lines
With grace and move toward
The wings. But the lines
Are awkward. Good-bye
Sticks in my throat—soliloquies
Have never been my forte.

The scene today is water
With the sun about to set;
The boats are slapping gently
At the dockside, where they're tied.
How wrong it seems that voices
Do not ring from children
Wading out to take the oars.
The catfish and the crappies
In the shallows come to feed.
How strange there is no boy
With a pole and bait.

The script notes say my voice
Should sound relieved,
Now that I'm finally freed
To move at will.
But this role wasn't made for me.
It's not an easy part.
I just can't get the hang of it.
Perhaps, I never will.

Gloria Gaither

The Shepherd Friend

The sheep may know the pasture,
But the Shepherd knows the sheep;
The sheep lie down in comfort,
But the Shepherd does not sleep.

He protects the young and foolish,
From their unprecocious way,
And gently prods the aged,
Lest they give in to the clay.

When the young have learned some wisdom,
It is much too late to act;
When the old man knows the method,
He is less sure of the fact.

Ah, the Shepherd knows the answer—
The beginning and the end.
So the wisest choice, my daughter,
Is to take him as your friend.

Dorothy Sickal

I

I knew a man
Who picked up a pencil
And drew around himself
A box
With well defined lines
And sharp edges
And I heard him swear
When he couldn't get out.

Suzanne Gaither at twenty

With Suzanne, age 14

With Amy, age 9, and Perdita

Mother with Suzanne, age 13

With Bill

Photo by Sue Buchanan

At 9

At 17

Photos by Nancy Copyright 1986

Photos by Nancy
Amy

At 8

Nancy's ©

Sue Buchanan

With Mother by our creek

Mother at our family cookout by our creek

Senior in
High School

Photos by Nancy
Suzanne

At 14

At 13

Spring House

Photos by Nancy

With Amy

Photos by Nancy

No Man Is an Island

I am affected.
At all times,
I affect,
And I am affected.
Does not a portion of me die
When a butterfly is killed,
When a star falls,
When the tide ebbs,
When a season changes,
When a brother departs?
Do I not die a little, too,
When a dream fades,
When a heart bears pain?
When a tear falls
And the soul is imprisoned,
Does my heart not feel pain?
Does my soul not cry out?
And what of joy?
Do not the power and potency of joy
Penetrate barriers of life and death,
Born and unborn,
Past and present?
No man is an island;
No man can hurt without hurting,
Feel without causing others to feel,
Rejoice without joining the stars in joy-song. . . .
No living being lives alone,
And Separated,
We are not at all.

Amy Gaither at seventeen

For a Cynic

There are those who die before the grave,
Who saunter on the sidelines
Plucking pilgrims from their courses
Which lead into horizons
That bend to kiss the ground.
They wander without motion
And without want for any,
Lashing out at those pursuing
An open, unknown sky—
They lie and speak the limitless in pounds.
Their boxes, neat and tidy,
Are all that lie beside them,
Categorically arranged
So nothing's gained and nothing's lost.
There are those who die before the grave,
Not knowing life has happened
They choose their death by dying
And all the while denying
They have counted everything . . .
Except the cost.

Suzanne Gaither at twenty-one

Minus One

I think of you, sitting by the fire,
Coffee mug beside you,
Letters spread out on your lap.
The dogs lie quietly at your feet,
Stretched out in private dreams.
I smell hot apple cider,
And vegetable soup simmering on the stove.
The clock is ticking on the mantle,
And the world is silent on this November afternoon;
The gray mist outside is held at bay
By our warm walls—
And I am not there to see you.
But I know you—
And when I close my eyes,
And feel you missing me, as I miss you,
Home is not so very far away.

                    Amy Gaither at eighteen

Seasons of
Celebration

January 5, 1984

The cold has broken
And so has the New Year,
Nineteen-eighty-four.
What's more, George Orwell
Was only partly right:
Big Brother's taken over half the globe,
But I am still in charge of me!
And love still reigns
Where simple hearts surrender
To its sovereignty
And stand up to refuse
The lords of earth.
Children still are running,
Singing in the streets,
And somewhere music still is floating
On the breeze at break of day.
There are some still looking for and finding
Lovely ways to serve their brothers,
And institutions have yet to take the place
Of mother-love and nurture.
There are homes across this land,
Still Nature's habitat
For fledgling humankind.
And folks still find
There's joy and warmth in friendship
And a smile.
The miles still wend their way
Across the amber waves of grain,
And purple mountains, still majestic,
Lift our sights
From the mundane and ordinary
To call us to keep reaching for our dreams.
And there are streams somewhere
From which it still is safe to drink
The water, flowing crystal

From the summit snow.
And while it is so
That wars are rumored all throughout the world
And flags unfurled are spat upon
And burned in effigy,
Still peace and blessed tranquility
Are here—within these walls
And in our hearts.

Gloria Gaither

March

An old fashioned March
With a newfangled twist;
Fickle, pushy, crafty, and brisk
Are some of the traits
On its character list.
Wind blows up your dress
And slides down your sleeve;
Indecent old rascal!
I just wish you'd leave.

Dorothy Sickal

Mobility

The open door before me,
White and foggy gusty winds,
A temporal situation
Is beginning once again.
For the stepping stones we follow,
Hard and round though small they seem,
Run on endless as a river
Fed by many struggling streams.
Looking hard for solid objects—
Mere illusions light the way—
White and black they see me wander
As I walk into their gray
Murky waters ripple outward,
Noiseless circles without rhyme—
Rounds of steady rhythms beating
Into some eternal time.
Opportunists call it treasure;
Faithful martyrs call it strife,
But the Word rings through the heavens,
And the poets call it life!

Suzanne Gaither at twenty

Joy

I hear people moaning about
How hard it is to be a parent.
They say that kids
Get in the way,
Cost too much,
And cause a lot of trouble.
They say they never would have had kids
If they'd known
What they know now.
Well, I'll confess
I'm very blessed,
For you have brought me
Only joy.
Well, not joy ONLY,
(I'll take that back).
You've brought me
Noise and arguments,
Drums and horns,
An aching back,
Pounding rhythms overhead,
And sandy grit beneath my feet,
Some sticky jelly on the wall,
And fingerprints along the hall,
And never, never can I find
An open phone line,
Combs with teeth,
A lid for toothpaste,
The playroom neat . . .

But back to what I said at first;
You've brought me joy.
First and last and in between,
The crazy days are always filled
With JOY!

Gloria Gaither

Nantucket

I can feel the ocean air from the jetties
Catching my hair and whipping it about my face
As I squint at the glare
Of the noon sun on the sea.
The water lapping around my ankles is cold,
But I shiver because I love this place.

I smell the home-made ice cream and cones
When I walk in the door;
The ceiling fans of the Sweet Shoppe
Stir the warm air and toss the smells out
Into the street.

I can hear the cry of the gulls
And feel the sun on my head and back,
While I bike down the long stretches
Of roads along the sea.
How I love the sea!
The wild grasses reach out
To brush against my legs
As they push the pedals that push my bike
Against the wind from the ocean.

I can see the tourists and university students,
Insensitive, impatient, and brash.
The children act like their parents,
And I turn away because I spot an islander,
Quiet, tolerant, and wise;
He has learned to deal with these intruders
From Boston and New York . . .
"Give them June and July—
Spring, fall, and winter are still ours."

Please—I'm different.
I love the island as you do;
Please recognize me.
I'm one of *you*.

I may never come back.
I may.
It doesn't matter.
I can close my eyes
And be here again—
Alone, with the sea and the wind and the gulls,
A native in this place.

Amy Gaither at fifteen

Who Hath Made Thee?

Who hath made thee, little lamb?
My heart you hold in fragile hand;
Your broken bird-like "coo" and "caw"
Speak wordless mystery to awe
   And touch my soul.

Pink-tipped fingers grip me fast
And cause cheap pleasures of the past
To wither like a worthless reed,
The offspring of self-centered greed,
   And leave me whole.

Who could look into your face
With its sweet essences of grace,
Total trust, and angelic smile
Of innocence and artless style,
   And be the same?

Surely, God hath sent you here
To whisper in my earthen ear
Of heaven's purity, my goal,
Lest I should wreck his gift, my soul,
   In worldly soil.

You, a cup of water pure,
Will man pollute thee, Satan lure
Away from thy high purpose here,
And stain thy joy with scalding tear?
   By my life, No!

God hath made thee, little lamb,
To walk with him on Golden Strand!
I dedicate me to that end,
And gladly, I, my life will spend
   To make it so!

Dorothy Sickal

Simplicity

I saw her there.
As breaking waves
Dashed around her little feet.
She laughed again
And dashed at them
Her eyes so full
She could not take it in
(Not all at once at least)
But breathe she did
Until her tiny lungs
Would burst with all the air
Then wild laughter broke into the wind.
For hours it seemed
The waves and she
Played their little game.
The sun had set without her knowing
And as I turned around to leave
I threw at her a final glance
At pigtails dancing in the sand.

Oh, to throw myself at sea
And drown in the immensity
My wish to thrust into the waves
A simple trust,
  A simple love,
    A simple joy of simple days.

       Suzanne Gaither at twenty-one

This Day

There is beauty in the morning
With the sun tip-toeing in,
When the day's a band new conscience,
And the world's a chance to win.

There is muscle in the noontime
When the sun is plowing through,
Hot and bright and clear and brawny,
Nature's time to go and do.

There's a charm about the evening—
Gentle, loving like a friend,
Smiling o'er the west horizon,
Tying up the day's loose ends.

Lovely, complicated wrappings
Sheathe the gift of one-day-more;
Breathless, I untie the package—
Never lived *this* day before!

Gloria Gaither

All My Fountains

Joy spring,
Bubble forth with laughter
And solemn joy,
Cleanse, renew.
We come, wretched, searching,
Every one of us,
And in being cleansed,
We will sing—
Joy song!
We will make music—
Joy song!
And as we make music,
We will sing,
"All my fountains are in you."

Joy spring,
Bubble forth
And cleanse us with your laughter.

Amy Gaither at eighteen

To Life

Summer was never so sweet!
To taste the fullest tang
And cut into the umbilical cord of life
A lush illusion, solidified and clear,
To rip the ripened vine
From rich and fertile soil
And let the roots become mine
Was all it took.
Every cell,
Rushing through pulsating streams
Stripped of man-made barriers;
So fresh and clean
The raging winter could not restrain
Green blossoms bursting out in me—
With natal eyes I scream
*L'chaiim!**

                    Suzanne Gaither at twenty

*"To life!" (Hebrew)

Renewal

I

I sit by the water
And wait for a wave to cover
my bare toes.
I spread my fingers in the sand
And feel time being cleansed
by these tiny crystals—
Old hurts, slipping away,
irretrievably.

II

Kahlil said the ocean laughs with
the innocent;
Maybe only the innocent hear
the ocean's laughter.
Maybe only the innocent laugh.

III

Cleanse me, vast sea;
Bring your peace to me.
Laugh, calm sea;
Laugh, and let me hear you—
Laugh, and let me laugh, too.

Amy Gaither at seventeen

The Woods Say Yes

The woods are full of sound,
And every sound a yes,
Affirming what I am,
Affirming that I am.
Let men invent their "no" machinery,
Grinding up incentive,
Blowing up the skies;
But nature's had her say,
And she says yes.
Let earth's bald cranium
Shake its defiant head
Until it rattles all our teeth—
The woods have heard their answer
From the Top—
The answer's yes.
We are. And evermore
Shall be.

Gloria Gaither

I Love the Rebel

I love the rebel,
The cripple, the thief—
The one who can look in the face
Of his grief—
The loner, the lover,
The poet whose song
Has lived through the fire,
Yet rises up strong.
I love all the dreamers
Who see more than things,
Who love both the bird
And the song that it sings.
A Robinhood person,
I settle the score
'Tween rich mediocre
And renegade poor.

Suzanne Gaither at twenty

The Englishman

He walked in, swinging his black cane,
His long, black coattail flapping,
Whistling some old English melody.
His pointed white beard touched
The bright red rose in his buttonhole
As he bowed gallantly to the dinner guests,
Swinging his tall hat gracefully
From his head to his heart
And back again.
I knew before he spoke
That he was an Englishman.
He strolled to the hostess,
Delicately kissed her hand,
And nodded politely.
He still did not speak.
He repeated this gesture
To a few of the other women
And shook hands with the men.
Then he waltzed over to me.
He was smiling sweetly,
With a twinkle in his eye,
And he reminded me of St. Nicholas.
He bent down to me
And took my hand in his
And looked straight
Into my blue, wondering eyes,
And said to me in a clean English accent,
"Merry Christmas"
And winked.

                    Amy Gaither at thirteen

"Even in Autumn" . . . The Promise

I went outside to hang up clothes
And saw the sky ablaze;
I turned to set the basket down
And saw the valley haze—
Its low-hung fog and purple dew
Of cool, damp autumn days.

I heard soft honking of wild geese,
The hunter's hated gun,
The accusations of a jay,
And saw a pheasant run!
Why must the evils of the earth
Throw shadows o'er God's sun?

The sad, sweet pageantries of fall
Reached out to twist my heart;
Old age and winter—hand in hand—
Stood o'er the hill, apart.
I grasped a pussy-willow bough—
'Twas budded! (What a start!)

Dorothy Sickal

Ode to Autumn

O autumn, thou hast robbed me
Of my senses,
Drained from me life and breath
With all thy beauty!
I should have stopped my ears
When first I heard thee
Calling gently through the frosty air.
But, O, how sweetly
Beckoned me, thy siren's song.
One note, my ears were thine.

My eyes I should have blinded
When first I glimpsed
A petal etched in tawny brown.
But wide-eyed as a child,
I watched as you began your promenade
Down forest trails,
And at your touch I saw the world transformed
To festivals of color
And saw the leaves begin to fall
Like wine and citron nectar drops
To fragrant pools below.

By now I could not turn my eyes away,
Nor could I stop my ears
Nor seal my senses from your pungent scent,
But then and there dismissed my will
And yielded
To your sweet embrace.

Gloria Gaither

They Kick the Face of Beauty

They kick the face of beauty
And spit upon her feet
And waste her priceless treasures
While they save their useless treats.

They buy and sell her body
Caring nothing for her soul
To gain a piece of silver
Just to reach a yearly goal.

They fail to see the loveliness
Of oceans and blue skies.
They chop away the forests
With blinders on their eyes.

But when a race is dying
She'll never hear their moans.
Then the lovely hair of beauty
Will grow up between their bones.

Suzanne Gaither at nineteen

Images

I have visions of sugar plums.
Purple and white
Frosting
Blonde curls
And white lace
Sparkles and sequins
Pudding and cakes.

Clara got a nutcracker.

Christmas parties
Velvet and satin
Red, green, pink
And white
Laughter
Fire and dancing
Lights on a tree.

Cavalier killed the Mouse King.

Crystal angels
Silvered mirrors
Crocheted ornaments
Golden balls
Reflecting light
Wooden soldiers
And a star.

The Snow Queen was white and beautiful.

Packages
Red and green
Ribbons
And bows
Piled beneath the tree
Silent
And waiting.

Sugar Plum Fairy danced with the Cavalier.

Diamonds
Sapphires
Gold
And silver
Frankincense
Myrrh
And beauty

Every wish Clara ever had—
Came true.

I have visions of sugar plums

They dance. . . .

                    Amy Gaither at seventeen

Seasons of Believing

Go and Make Disciples

"Go and make disciples,"
Said the Master to his men.
"Go and find the lost and homeless
And gently bring them in."

"We will do it!" shouted Peter.
"We will seek them far and wide."
"He said 'gently,' " meek John cautioned,
"Better take a steady stride.
Let us pray and ask the Spirit
If he'll lead us as we go,
Lest we be more harm than blessing
And be ruined by the foe."

"Oh, I doubt if we can do it,"
Mumbled Thomas through his fears.
"Folks don't want to follow Jesus. . . .
We've been working here for years."
"We can never be defeated,"
With assurance Phillip said.
Confident in mind and conduct,
He had tasted living bread.

Judas lagged behind in protest,
Looking darkly at the others.
In his heart was greed and gossip
And no love for Christ or brothers.
"There is time enough," he stated
To the others as they went;
In his practiced sly and cunning,
Who could tell just what he meant?

James, the willing "son of thunder"
Always ready in his heart,
Trusting in the Master, answered,

"Now's the perfect time to start."
Andrew looked upon the distance,
Saw the needs out in the field:
"We can win them all, my brothers,
Since his will has been revealed."

So they all went out together,
Filled with hope and faith and love;
One rebelled, another doubted,
But God helped them from above.
Thomases are always doubting;
Judases are here to stay,
Who, while others make disciples,
Try to find some easy way.

Yet the Savior leads his people,
Makes disciples of the poor,
As the ages keep on rolling
Gives assurance o'er and o'er.
When the books of life are opened,
Honors given for the race,
Those who went and made disciples
Will be those to see his face.

Dorothy Sickal

Child's Prayer

You have always been my life—
Not just a part of it,
For I am a part of you.
I remember
A dimly lit room
With yellow curtains—
A child's room—
And a child
With yellow hair
Kneeling at a chair,
Enfolded by her mother's loving arms.
She said a prayer;
It was a child's prayer—
A prayer that has sustained me
And given me love.
My life in this house
With these people, my family,
Has always been centered
On you—
Making life beautiful,
But not easy.
I run blindly at times
In the mazes I create for myself,
And in those
Others have created for me;
You are at none of the ends;
I only find you
When I look up.

How many times can I run,
Crying
Into your arms,
Thanking you and promising "never again"?
Since I have nothing else,
Though it seems not enough—

My eternal forgiver,
Friend,
Father,
And strength—
I give to you, once again,
My life.

May it be pleasing to you, Father.
And may I always strive
To maintain it for you,
Clean and pure,
Acceptable.
Help me to come to you first,
Not as a last resort,
But as the first, last, and only
Answer.

I am still that child—
Yours—
And I love you.

Amy Gaither at fifteen

I Mean Before

I hugged you tight
And felt the muscles ripple
In your sturdy little shoulders.
"I love you, Benj," I said.
"I sure am glad we had you."
You smiled as if to say
That you're glad, too.
"Mom?" you asked,
And pulled me back,
"Are there babies somewhere waiting
Who never will be born?"
"What do you mean?" I asked.
"Do you mean babies
Who get sick or die
Or never grow quite big enough to live?"
"No," you answered.
"I mean is there a place
Where babies wait
Before they come to be,
And if no one wants them
Or love that makes them start . . .
Are they left to go on waiting
Never to be born,
Never, ever come to be
A boy like me?"
"Why do you ask?"
I answered with a question.
(A mother's skilled at answers
That don't answer
And questions that don't question
Real questions of the heart.)
"Because I have a feeling,"
You said with childish wisdom,
"That I've been going on

A long, long time,
And I will keep on going
Even after all of us are gone.
And I'm sure glad
That I came to be your kid—
That you and Daddy love me.
I caught a bass today.
Good-night."

Gloria Gaither

Isaac

I laid myself upon the altar
To be sacrificed
Not in part, but in whole.
I gave all that I could call my own
My love, my talents, my identity
And life so full
And yet so empty
I gave all.
My eyes swelled full
A frightened child
I watched
For that freeing, fatal stroke
Remembering through the tears
The cause
The cause
And past the cause, the Power
The Power that called into my soul
Called soul away from body
And falling fast
I know I died.
At last
Immortal, natal eyes
Upward turned
Beheld the Lamb.

Suzanne Gaither at twenty

When I Think of You

Do you know what you remind me of?
The warm summer sun of early evening,
Sending its soft rays right down to where I am,
Touching my cheek and caressing me with its brilliance—
You,
Who makes the sun shine.

Do you know what you remind me of?
The white moon, piercing through the darkness of night,
Being quiet in its wisdom and royalty,
Laughing silently—
You,
Who brings light in the midst of darkness.

Do you know what you remind me of?
The billions of tiny, blinking stars,
Thousands of times bigger in reality,
Dancing childlike across the sky,
Oblivious to problems—
You,
Who joins in the song of the stars and brings it to me.

Do you know what you remind me of?
The great, sparkling ocean,
Never ending,
Providing life to sustain,
Frightening in its vastness and depth,
And yet alluring—
You,
Who brings me calm serenity.

You,
Who gives me life.

Amy Gaither at thirteen

"The Popular Consecration"
(A Parody)

I'll go where you want me to go, dear Lord,
    If it happens to fit my plan;
I'll be what you want me to be, dear Lord,
    When I've done everything that I can
To make myself comfortable, healthy, and rich,
    And my barns big enough for the needs;
I'd like to go out and win others to Christ,
    But my garden's so cluttered with weeds!

I've prayed and I've read your blessed old Book;
    I love the great sermons and songs.
I enjoy the good feeling when I meet with the saints,
    But don't ask me to work too long.
Yes, I'll go where you want me to go, dear Lord,
    I have carefully planned my course.
When I've done all the things that I want to do,
    I'll do more for you—of course.

I'll say what you want me to say, dear Lord,
    To those in the clutches of sin,
And I'll be at the church when I ask them to come,
    If relatives don't drop in.
I'll say what you want me to say, dear Lord,
    When I've said what I've fixed up to say
To that preacher or teacher who fails to do
    The work of the church in my way!

I would go, I would be, I would say, dear Lord,
    What my heart tells me I should
If others would do their part, too, dear Lord;
    So often I've prayed that they would.
I've done so much for your work here, Lord,
    But nobody seems to care;
If they would appreciate me as they should,
    I'd work just anywhere.

But I'd rather preach than sweep, dear Lord,
  And I'd rather sing than pray.
And I'll do anything, dear Lord,
  If I can only have my way.
I can't understand it at all, dear Lord,
  When I think of a harp and a crown
And I kneel down to pray for other folks
  I somehow feel "let down."

I would stay where you want me to stay, dear Lord,
  But I've made up my mind to go.
There is work to be done everywhere, dear Lord,
  And workers are few, you know.
I want you to lead me each day, dear Lord,
  And have your way in my heart.
I guess you've found out I'm a pretty good guy;
I knew that I was from the start.

Dorothy Sickal

If You Had Been There!

An empty house where laughter once had rung . . .
An child's room vacant except for one
broken toy . . .
A brown bottle in a dusty corner, silent
symbol of a ruthless tyrant . . .

O Lord, if you had been there . . . !

Once-human voices bemoaning some
"unpardonable sin" . . .
Sane façades miserably betrayed by
insane eyes and hands . . .
The sterile corridors of a sterile hell . . .

O Lord, if you had been there . . . !

The sickening brown and red of mud and blood . . .
Young thighs, twisted and bullet-ridden . . .
A conference table encircled by fat,
unyielding faces . . .

O Lord, if you had been there . . . !

An aged child scurrying into an alley with stolen
loot . . .
A brick-strewn street lined with angry faces . . .
A weeping mother bending over a
blue-uniformed corpse . . .

O Lord, if you had been there . . . !

The silence of words never uttered . . .
The silence of no words to utter . . .
The silence that follows too many words,
too quickly uttered . . .

O Lord, if you had been there . . . !

Gloria Gaither

On the Lord's Day

Aren't you glad for the house of prayer?
We meet our Lord and our neighbors there!
What sweet tranquility fills the day,
When we enter the church in a worshipful way.

We watch the coming of some little boy,
His face all scrubbed and beaming with joy,
And we think as we watch him, "Here comes a man
Who will serve his God the best he can."

The smiling girl in ruffle and pleat,
And the soft-voiced ladies, kind and sweet,
And the stately gentlemen with soft, white hair
All congregate and are waiting there.

I wouldn't miss it for world's unknown!
This chance again to approach the "throne"
And bow with my friends and unload my care
At the feet of Jesus in the house of prayer.

Dorothy Sickal

Dim

Somebody turn on the light . . .
I cannot see.
It is dark and cold.
Ouch!
Another weight just fell on me.
I can't bear this.
Turn your eyes upon Jesus.
God! Where are you?
I can't even find you.
O love that will not let me go . . .
This tunnel is getting smaller,
And I'm not sure if there's an end.
I'm not really sure about anything.
Everything here is so scary.
Fear not. Rest in me.
God! Are you even there?
Are you anywhere?
I am no longer angry
Or impatient.
I am numb
And afraid
And alone. . . .
And the things of Earth will grow strangely dim . . .
My heart is a cold stone
That is getting smaller.
Can stones cry?
Oh, my soul!
I rest my weary soul in thee . . .
Dreams . . . I cannot dream
Because they will never come true.
God! What is the point?
Why aren't you . . . Why can't you . . . ?
I am the great I am. I am Jehovah.
I am the Lord.

Thou shalt love the Lord your God
With ALL your heart.
But I can't feel my heart.
I can't see . . .
I can't turn my eyes upon Jesus;
I can't lift my eyes unto the hills;
I can't.
In the light of His glory and grace.
The sun shall not smite thee by day,
Nor the moon by night.
Bless the Lord
O, my soul!
And ALL that is within me,
Bless his holy name.
And the things of Earth will grow
Strangely dim. . . .

Amy Gaither at sixteen

"Deus Venerunt Gentes"*

We have violated the face of God.
Building Disneylands to appease
Our hedonistic natures,
We have squandered all we owe.
Power has become the joy of our ascent
As we bite again and again Eve's poison fruit.
It's no wonder that the heavy serpent
Has curved its naked body
Around our modern Babel
And caught us in its gaping jaws
As we have fallen.
When will we speak no longer
In the dream that rationalizes our fabricated morality—
When will we "learn that the vessel that the serpent broke
WAS AND IS NOT:
And let the guilty know
That God's own vengeance
Has no fear of sops"?

Suzanne Gaither at twenty-two

*Translated: "O God, the heathen are come." The final quotation is also from Dante's
Purgatory.

A Going Home

The weary sun
   cools mellow in the west
   and calls to me
      to find a place where I can rest.
And like the sun
   I long to find
      an old familiar path that winds
      its way back to a place
Where they're expecting me
   and I can be
      where I belong.

The sounds I hear—
   The voices that I know so well—
   The laughter and the music,
   The children so excited to be first
      to tell the most amusing
      thing that happened
Since we walked into the morning,
      went our separate ways.

Without a doubt I know it:
   The table will be set,
   And there will be a place for me
   Just where I always sit
   There, just across from Father
      by the window.
Before I even get there
   I can smell the fire
   burning in the kitchen,
And the cold that chills me to the bone
      somehow knows the warmth is coming
      and lets go of me.

As much as I anticipate
  the faces loved so well,
  I long to find a place to be alone
    When I get home.
Solitude:
  a place and time to think;
  a chance to drink in all the joy that I have
known;
  a room all my own.
For I plan to go on growing,
  secure in knowing
    I am loved . . .
      and I am home.

Gloria Gaither

Come and See Me

I tried to tell my friends about
The beauties of the hills.
I talked about the ocean,
And how it rolls and spills,
But they only yawned and murmured,
"That must be nice to see."
  So I said—
"If you ever want to go there,
  Come and see me!"

I described the profound joys
That I felt down in my soul
As I stood in a sun-drenched valley
And watched old Jordan roll.
But my friends had other interests;
They were listless as could be.
  But I said—
"If you ever want to go there,
  Come and see me!"

I might not have seen the ocean
Had a friend not drawn me there,
Talked all about its vastness,
Its great beauty tried to share.
When I could not catch the vision,
He so kindly said to me,
"If you ever want to go there,
  Come and see me!"

If you want to meet my Jesus,
Find your place in God's great plan
When your heart is filled with longing
To be the person that you can.
If your sins become too heavy.

And you ache in misery,
When you want a friend to help you,
I'll be glad to introduce you,
    Come and see me!

Dorothy Sickal

To the Naturalist

How, humble man, can you look
At a bird in a tree
Or tall grass, growing in the
    shallow water,
Or listen to the crickets at
    night;
How can you see and hear these things,
And not see and hear God?

How, solitary man, can you watch
Tiny water insects dart across
    the surface of a pond
Or feel the breeze on your face
Or smell the pines above your head;
How can you see and feel and smell these things,
And not see and feel and smell God?

How, sensitive man, can you hold a
    small bird in your heart
And shun your brother;
How can you so love nature
And ignore the Creator?
How can you recognize the beautiful
And deny the Source of beauty?
How, O Naturalist,
Can you not recognize the God
Who made these things—
Who made even the brother that you shun?

For how can you live
And touch
And hear
And see
But by God?

Amy Gaither at sixteen

Consumed

I couldn't stop the flame
So out of obligation
I ran again to meet it
To give the blaze a name
To call into the tongues
The Word for which it yearned
And like a wild animal tamed
Returned to Womb from which it came
And sorrow filled my heart
For something died
And something born.

Suzanne Gaither at twenty

Renascence

There's no darkness quite so black
  as darkness seen by eyes that never open,
    have not seen the sun.
Life to the unborn is filled with little
  but a void. I know
    for I am one
      yet unborn.
        Oh, I am one!

Yet something deep inside me keeps on reaching
  through the darkness,
    pushing back despair,
      black despair—
        hope is there.

The seed of the divine, the simple, timeless
  knowing there must be a place
    I could be growing,
      is compelling me,
        expelling me . . .

Longing for the dawning of the soul of me,
  I risk the pain of recreation
    and the agony
      of my nativity.
I leave the cozy womb of my mortality,
  rushing headlong to eternity
    willingly, willingly!

And I'm alive again!
  I'm a child again!
    I am walking unashamed and naked
      in a brand new world,
        and I'm wide-eyed again!

Clean inside again!
And I can see!
Oh,
    I can see!

Gloria Gaither

The Mingling

Just a happy time together
With the children of the Lord
When we mingle with our loved ones,
Brought together by his Word.

Yet there is a note of sadness;
There are faces here tonight
Who will not be long among us
Will be hidden from our sight.

But there is a joy in knowing—
He who guides the little star
Will take care of all his children,
Makes no difference where they are!

This wide earth, which looks so mammoth
To us little folks down here,
Is but a tiny speck of matter
To the eyes of Father dear!

Prayer can reach from earth to glory,
He can answer anywhere
All the needs of all his people,
Whether they be far or near.

Let us then rejoice together,
In this fellowship recline!
Let not distance, time, or sorrow
Break apart our love divine.

Dorothy Sickal

The Garment

And having gone so far
   into that immense desert
   without drink,
   without warmth,
   wanting . . .
I saw the form of a tattered Garment
   hanging from a tree.
The force of long-lamented iniquity
   and arid need
   thrust my weakened, shaking hand
   toward that crimson thing.
So ghostly white
   my battered knuckles were
   that I could hardly close
   my empty hand to grasp.

Slowly,
   trembling whiteness
   extending,
   stretching,
   longing for Substance
   reached away from
   a lifeless form
   into the depths of that
   crimsoned Garment.

Suddenly . . .
   bleached skin touched velvet;
   blood rushed over parched bone;
   flooded arteries,
   filled veins.
With all my strength,

I clutched desperately that empowering lifeforce
    until. . . . A voice,
    commanding and compassionate,
    called into the windless desert,
        Who touched me?
And I,
    knowing the Source from which it came,
    fell prostrate on red ground
    and cried,
        "My Lord, my God,
            It was I."

                    Suzanne Gaither at twenty-one

Yes to Something Higher

Saying "no" may mean
    that I've said "yes" to something higher;
Pleasure for a season
    cannot buy eternity.
Joy and lasting peace and deep contentment
    are a treasure
That no cheap thrills or easy rides
    will trick from me.

Saying "no" to lesser men
    means I've said "yes" to Jesus.
I am very careful whom I choose to call
    "My Lord."
I will gladly wash your feet
    or offer any service
Bowing only to the love
    found in his Word.

Markets of the world
    may bid to make me easy barter,
But I refuse to sell myself
    in bits and pieces.
Noisy vendors vie for my consent
    with second guesses,
But I will spend my "yeses"
    on things that never die.

When you sense a calling
    to the best that is within you;
When you know deep in your heart
    you've found a better way,

Turn your back on all the voices
    that would drag you downward;
Saying "no"
May be the grandest "yes"
    you'll ever say!

Gloria Gaither

A.D. *3/30*

In the stillness of dusk
A hush surrounded the olive trees;
The restless doves flew circles
Over the unrippled bay.
Underground, brown seeds rustled in brown dirt;
A grain of sand turned over on the beach;
A mother rabbit went into noiseless labor;
Giant flounder spawned on the shore.
The old fisherman
Anchored his worn boat to the dock
And dragged in the half-empty net.
A little boy sneezed,
A woman poured tea,
And a small group of men
Whispered words in the dark.

All was still.
All was shadowed.
All was expectant . . .
On Saturday night
  before Easter.

                    Suzanne Gaither at twenty

Revelation

I.   There was no use for dreams
In this barren land where we wept without tears,
Wept when we remembered . . .
The cracked ground knew the passing of time,
And clouds of dusty smoke
Were the only remnants of a much larger cloud.
It didn't matter now
Nor did the Russian names;
Nothing reigned over nothingness.
We walked around in gray
Much bleaker than any black or white
Where mirages of cities appeared and vanished.
Three copper pennies
With a shiny dullness
Lay on the ground.
Useless.

II.   "Absalom, my son,
For so long I have . . ."
His voice was as cracked
As the ground on which he walked.
He stumbled on,
Calling into the gray stench,
"Absalom!"
But nothing echoed back,
"Abba, Father."
He stumbled again
And called into the windless wind.

III.   In the valley where we walked
There were many carcasses
Of dry, parched bones. .
No wind blew now;
No armies marched.

We came upon the dead forms
Of six young sheep.
Who will save us?
Then in the distance something moved, alive.
Walking, walking
Closer, clearer
The seventh lamb,
Stopping beside the dead bodies,
Which were its brothers,
It began to weep a real tear.
A real tear touched the ground . . .
And then the wind blew.
We ascended.
Looking into the eyes
Of one lamb's lament,
"It is finished."
From where I stood
I saw the window
Of an old church,
The ripped curtain
Flowing in the wind.
"It is finished."
The lamb bowed its head
And Spirit ascended.
Oh, Eliot,*
It did end with a bang.
It did,
Until Rachel** cried.

Suzanne Gaither at twenty-one

---

*Eliot—In the poem "The Hollow Men" by T. S. Eliot, the end of the world comes "not with a bang but a whimper."
**Rachel—(Jer. 31:15).

Apocalypse in Hindsight

It began with no ado—
The fig tree always blossoms,
So that was nothing new.
The sky was filled with wonders,
But wonders are the norm
To those who've learned to see.
There was a holy hush,
Now that you mention it,
A stillness like the sound
Of marrow in the bone,
Regenerating life and sending out
Red cells to slither down
The cylinders so small.
I guess we should have known—
The moon that funny color
Like sun at six o'clock—
But we'd grown accustomed to
The tricks the atmosphere can play,
Polluted by the progress man has made.
Yes, now I do recall
A far-off sound
Like some musician tuning
In the practice room backstage.
But I see this all
In hindsight; I really
Didn't notice what was happening
Until the trumpet blew.

Gloria Gaither

In a Word

As blood sprang forth from the root
The Universe erupted a radiant lava,
Spreading silently over creeping life.

The beauty, bathed in the passionate heat,
Stood spectrally, refreshed and renewed.

Red cylinders spun their way around the
Cracked planet
Dripping crimson into dehydrated mire

And on that day

All was encased in warm, red dew

Perhaps to please a cynic
Perhaps to please some esoteric elite
Perhaps to please . . .

Suzanne Gaither at twenty-one

ADDITIONAL COPYRIGHT INFORMATION

(Continued from copyright page)

Seasons of Becoming

"Old Lady Grisemar" copyright © 1988 by Dorothy Sickal; "Branches" copyright © 1988 by Amy Gaither; "Aspirations" copyright © 1988 by Suzanne Gaither; "You Walked So Straight" copyright © 1988 by Gloria Gaither; "To Be an Artist" copyright © 1988 by Amy Gaither; "To Be a Dreamer" copyright © 1988 by Gloria Gaither; "One Mother's Prayer" copyright © 1983 by Dorothy Sickal; "Union of Poles" copyright © 1988 by Suzanne Gaither; "Identity" copyright © 1988 by Gloria Gaither; "Perception" copyright © 1988 by Amy Gaither; "Of Course! (for Benjy)" copyright © 1988 by Dorothy Sickal; "Oasis" copyright © 1988 by Amy Gaither; "Hope" copyright © 1988 by Gloria Gaither; "The Void" copyright © 1988 by Suzanne Gaither; "Progeria" copyright © 1988 by Gloria Gaither; "Equilibrium" copyright © 1988 by Amy Gaither; "To Know a Heart" copyright © 1988 by Suzanne Gaither; "The Pilgrim" copyright © 1988 by Gloria Gaither; "Peripeteia" copyright © 1988 by Suzanne Gaither; "Metamorphosis" copyright © 1988 by Gloria Gaither; "Alone" copyright © 1988 by Suzanne Gaither; "Is This All?" copyright © 1988 by Dorothy Sickal; "Waters" copyright © 1988 by Amy Gaither; "There Are No Puppies" copyright © 1988 by Suzanne Gaither.

Seasons of Relationships

"I Like Being Married to You" copyright © 1988 by Gloria Gaither; "Who Is It?" copyright © 1988 by Suzanne Gaither; "To Whom It May Concern" copyright © 1988 by Amy Gaither; "One and One Make One" copyright © 1988 by Gloria Gaither; "You" copyright © 1988 by Suzanne Gaither; "The Fighter" copyright © 1988 by Gloria Gaither; "Intuition" copyright © 1988 by Suzanne Gaither; "To My Mother" copyright © 1988 by Amy Gaither; "Sibling" copyright © 1988 by Amy Gaither; "To Our Daughter" copyright © 1988 by Dorothy Sickal; "Left" copyright © 1988 by Amy Gaither; "At the Last" copyright © 1988 by Suzanne Gaither; "The Glory" copyright © 1988 by Dorothy Sickal; "Time for Separating" copyright © 1988 by Gloria Gaither; "Long Distance Leaf" copyright © 1988 by Suzanne Gaither; "Freshman, 1987" copyright © 1988 by Amy Gaither; "Little Nell" copyright © 1988 by Dorothy Sickal; "Sunshine" copyright © 1988 by Gloria Gaither; "To My Gracious Mother" copyright © 1988 by Suzanne Gaither; "I Know a Lady" copyright © 1988 by Amy Gaither; "Value" copyright © 1988 by Gloria Gaither; "Miscast" copyright © 1988 by Gloria Gaither; "The Shepherd Friend" copyright © 1988 by Dorothy Sickal; "I" copyright © 1988 by Suzanne Gaither; "No Man Is an Island" copyright © 1988 by Amy Gaither; "For a Cynic" copyright © 1988 by Suzanne Gaither; "Minus One" copyright © 1988 by Amy Gaither.

Seasons of Celebration

"January 5, 1984" copyright © 1988 by Gloria Gaither; "March" copyright © 1988 by Dorothy Sickal; "Mobility" copyright © 1988 by Suzanne Gaither; "Joy" copyright © 1988 by Gloria Gaither; "Nantucket" copyright © 1988 by Amy Gaither; "Who Hath Made Thee?" copyright © 1988 by Dorothy Sickal; "Simplicity" copyright © 1988 by Suzanne Gaither; "This Day" copyright © 1988 by Gloria Gaither; "All My Fountains" copyright © 1988 by Amy Gaither; "To Life" copyright © 1988 by Suzanne Gaither; "Renewal" copyright © 1988 by Amy Gaither; "The Woods Say Yes" copyright © 1988 by Gloria Gaither; "I Love the Rebel" copyright © 1988 by Suzanne Gaither; "The Englishman" copyright © 1988 by Amy Gaither; "'Even in Autumn' . . . The

Promise" copyright © 1988 by Dorothy Sickal; "Ode to Autumn" copyright © 1988 by Gloria Gaither; "They Kick the Face of Beauty" copyright © 1988 by Suzanne Gaither; "Images" copyright © 1988 by Amy Gaither.

Seasons of Believing

"Go and Make Disciples" copyright © 1988 by Dorothy Sickal; "Child's Prayer" copyright © 1988 by Amy Gaither; "I Mean Before" copyright © 1988 by Gloria Gaither; "Isaac" copyright © 1988 by Suzanne Gaither; "When I Think of You" copyright © 1988 by Amy Gaither; "'The Popular Consecration' (A Parody)" copyright © 1988 by Dorothy Sickal; "If You Had Been There!" copyright © 1988 by Gloria Gaither; "On the Lord's Day" copyright © 1988 by Dorothy Sickal; "Dim" copyright © 1988 by Amy Gaither; "Deus Venerunt Gentes" copyright © 1988 by Suzanne Gaither; "A Going Home" copyright © 1988 by Gloria Gaither; "Come and See Me" copyright © 1988 by Dorothy Sickal; "To the Naturalist" copyright © 1988 by Amy Gaither; "Consumed" copyright © 1988 by Suzanne Gaither; "Renascence" copyright © 1988 by Gloria Gaither; "The Mingling" copyright © 1988 by Dorothy Sickal; "The Garment" copyright © 1988 by Suzanne Gaither; "Yes to Something Higher" copyright © 1988 by Gloria Gaither; "A.D. 3/30" copyright © 1988 by Suzanne Gaither; "Revelation" copyright © 1988 by Suzanne Gaither; "Apoclaypse in Hindsight" copyright © 1988 by Gloria Gaither; "In a Word" copyright © 1988 by Suzanne Gaither.